Sermon on the Mount
Leader Guide

D1596791

Sermon on the Mount
A Beginner's Guide to the Kingdom of Heaven
Leader Guide

Sermon on the Mount Leader Guide
978-1-5018-9991-1
978-1-5018-9992-8 eBook

Sermon on the Mount
978-1-5018-9989-8
978-1-5018-9990-4 eBook

Sermon on the Mount DVD
978-1-5018-9993-5

Also by Amy-Jill Levine

Entering the Passion of Jesus: A Beginner's Guide to Holy Week

Light of the World: A Beginner's Guide to Advent

AMY-JILL LEVINE

SERMON *on* *the* MOUNT

A BEGINNER'S GUIDE to the KINGDOM of HEAVEN

LEADER GUIDE

by Mike Poteet

Abingdon Press
Nashville

Sermon on the Mount
Leader Guide

Copyright © 2020 Amy-Jill Levine
All rights reserved.

ISBN 13: 978-1-5018-9991-1

20 21 22 23 24 25 26 27 28 29—10 9 8 7 6 5 4 3 2 1
MANUFACTURED IN THE UNITED STATES OF AMERICA

CONTENTS

INTRODUCTION

In *Sermon on the Mount*, Dr. Amy-Jill Levine (University Professor of New Testament and Jewish Studies, Vanderbilt Divinity School and College of Arts and Science) encourages all readers, both Christians and those outside Christian communions, to reexamine the Sermon on the Mount—the large block of Jesus's teachings found in chapters 5–7 of the Gospel of Matthew.

Recognizing how little most readers understand about Jesus's first-century Jewish context, Dr. Levine (who prefers to be called AJ) guides readers through the Sermon section by section, and in doing so helps them to read it "as a teaching given by one Jew to fellow Jews." As she has frequently noted: if we get Jesus's context wrong, we'll get him wrong. More, if we get the context right, we can find even more meaning in his words.

Without ever denying that the text is *more* than a historical artifact to Christian readers, AJ wisely and often quite winsomely insists that Christian readers must not treat it as *less*. The Sermon on the Mount is not only the Scripture of the church but also the teaching that made sense to the Jewish disciples who followed Jesus of Nazareth. To ignore that history means to miss the import of Jesus's words—words that provide instruction on how best to live into the kingdom of heaven (see Matthew 7:24-27). More, readers who ignore that context have, over the centuries, imported anti-Jewish interpretations into the Sermon and, thus, deformed the Gospel.

This Leader Guide is designed to help Christian adult education leaders shepherd a group through a six-session study of the Sermon on the Mount, a study informed by AJ's book. This guide contains quotations from her book that can serve as prompts for discussion, but groups will gain the most when the guide is accompanied by reading both Matthew 5–7 and AJ's *Sermon on the Mount*.

About the Sessions

Here is an overview of the six sessions in this leader guide:

- Session 1, "Introduction and the Beatitudes," orients participants to the Sermon as an introductory guide to the kingdom of heaven; it examines Jesus's statements about blessedness (the "Beatitudes") as indications of God's will for those who gather in Jesus's name in particular and for human life in general.
- Session 2, "The Extensions," helps participants appreciate the utmost seriousness with which Jesus took the Torah and the Prophets—that is, the Scriptures of Israel—and examines how the "fences" he built around God's Law to protect it enhance the lives of his followers, individually and communally, then and now.
- In session 3, "Practicing Piety," participants will both discover Jesus's views on the right and wrong ways to engage in expressions of faith and reflect on how appropriate practices can lead to peace with one another and within themselves.
- Session 4, "Our Father," looks at how the Lord's Prayer is a quintessentially Jewish prayer, reveals the historical nuances of the terms in each verse, and considers how its recitation can function as personal spiritual discipline, recognition of interpersonal reconciliation, and awareness of communal political and economic concerns.
- In session 5, "Finding Your Treasure," participants will reflect on and reevaluate their attitudes toward wealth, treasure, and "stuff," and will imagine how their lives and the world would be different were Jesus's teachings about these realities to prevail.
- In session 6, "Living into the Kingdom," participants will identify challenges to traveling along what Jesus called the "narrow

road" leading to life and will talk about ways along the journey in which the church community members can support one another as well as those who belong to other communities.

Each of the six session plans includes:

- Stated goals for you to keep in mind as you lead discussions.
- The printed text, from the New Revised Standard Version (NRSV), of the portion of the Sermon on the Mount discussed in that session. (A few sessions contain additional Scripture texts as well, and all sessions refer participants to other passages in several discussion questions.)
- Extensive discussion questions to facilitate participants' engagement with both the biblical text and AJ's book. You likely won't have the time or desire to use all of the questions; choose the ones most interesting or relevant to your group.
- Opening and closing prayers to ground your sessions in an atmosphere of worship.

Some sessions contain optional, easy-to-prepare, and easy-to-do activities to serve as icebreakers or interactive introductions to the session's topic. Each session's Leader Preparation notes will alert you to any extra materials you need or preparation to accomplish.

May God, in great grace, use this guide and your group's study to draw you closer into the life of the kingdom of heaven!

Session 1

THE BEATITUDES

Session Goals

This session's reading, discussion, reflection, and prayer will equip participants to:

- Appreciate how the Sermon on the Mount functions as an introductory guide to the kingdom of heaven.
- Consider how the Sermon on the Mount's immediate context shapes ways of reading and understanding it to better appreciate Matthew's narrative.
- Identify the beatitude form in Scripture and express what it means to be "blessed."
- Discuss Jesus's Beatitudes as expressions of God's will for human life.
- Refine and articulate their own understandings of the kingdom of heaven (each participant may well have a personal takeaway), informed by studying Jesus's Beatitudes.

Biblical Foundations

Jesus went throughout Galilee, teaching in their synagogues and proclaiming the good news of the kingdom and curing every disease and every sickness among the people. So his fame spread throughout all Syria, and they brought to him all the sick, those who were afflicted with various diseases and pains,

*demoniacs, epileptics, and paralytics, and he cured them.
And great crowds followed him from Galilee, the Decapolis,
Jerusalem, Judea, and from beyond the Jordan.*

*When Jesus saw the crowds, he went up the mountain; and
after he sat down, his disciples came to him. Then he began to
speak, and taught them, saying:*

*"Blessed are the poor in spirit, for theirs is the kingdom of
     heaven.*
"Blessed are those who mourn, for they will be comforted.
"Blessed are the meek, for they will inherit the earth.
*"Blessed are those who hunger and thirst for righteousness, for
     they will be filled.*
"Blessed are the merciful, for they will receive mercy.
"Blessed are the pure in heart, for they will see God.
*"Blessed are the peacemakers, for they will be called children
     of God.*
*"Blessed are those who are persecuted for righteousness' sake,
     for theirs is the kingdom of heaven.*
*"Blessed are you when people revile you and persecute you and
     utter all kinds of evil against you falsely on my account.
     Rejoice and be glad, for your reward is great in heaven, for
     in the same way they persecuted the prophets who were
     before you."*

Matthew 4:23–5:12

Suggested Leader Preparation

• Before your first session, set aside enough time to read the
  Sermon on the Mount (Matthew 5–7) in a single sitting, at
  least once. Read the chapters in more than one translation (for
  example, Common English Bible, King James Version, New
  American Bible Revised Edition, New International Version,
  New Revised Standard Version), including one you've never
  read before. Read these chapters aloud. Listen to them from
  an audio Bible. Make notes on the Sermon's major topics and

themes. Try outlining the chapters and summarizing them in your own words. The more you immerse yourself in the Sermon, the better prepared you will be to help participants study each of its parts in the context of the whole.

- Carefully and prayerfully read Matthew 4:23–5:12, making notes of whatever grabs your attention, sparks new questions, or provides new insights. If desired, consult a trusted Bible commentary after you have read and reflected on the text yourself.
- Carefully read the introduction and chapter 1 from *Sermon on the Mount* by Amy-Jill Levine. Note any material you need or want to research further before the session.
- Have on hand Bible dictionaries, concordances (or identify trusted online equivalents), a variety of Bible translations for participants to use (recommended), and pencils/pens and paper. If you are in touch with the people likely to join you for these sessions, invite them to bring their own Bibles. Optional: Gather an assortment of recent newspapers and magazines.
- If using the DVD or streaming video in your study, preview the session 1 segment and choose the best time in your session to view it.

As Your Group Gathers

Welcome participants. Ask them to introduce themselves and to talk briefly about what they hope to gain from this study of Amy-Jill Levine's *Sermon on the Mount*. Be ready to talk about your personal interest in and hopes for the study as well. Ask:

- When was a time you needed an introduction or "beginner's guide" to some subject or activity?
- What is one subject or activity for which you would be qualified to write a "beginner's guide?"
- Complete this sentence: "I'd really appreciate but have never found a beginner's guide to _____."

Introduce AJ to the group and ask if any participants are familiar with her work or have used any other of her Abingdon Bible Studies. Tell participants that she, in her book, reads Jesus's Sermon on the Mount as "a beginner's guide to the kingdom of heaven." Welcome them to interact with her comments, feel free to disagree with her, or to elaborate on her views: Bible study should be an opportunity to express diverse views.

Encourage participants to attend closely to Jesus's words during this study so that the Sermon on the Mount might shape or even shake up our understanding of what "the kingdom of heaven" is.

Pray this prayer or one in your own words:

> *O God, most holy and praised: As your Son gathered disciples to himself to teach them your ways, so your Spirit has gathered us in this time and place. Make us alert and attentive as we read and reflect on Jesus's words; help us take them to heart and live into them so that your will is truly done on earth as in heaven. We pray in the name of our true Teacher, Jesus Christ. Amen.*

Setting the Stage for the Sermon

Have participants open their Bibles to and spend a few minutes skimming Matthew 5–7. Ask:

- What topics or themes did you notice most as you skimmed these chapters?
- What parts of these chapters, if any, struck you as familiar or unfamiliar?
- AJ writes, "The Sermon on the Mount is not a sermon; it's a series of discrete teachings. . . . Had Jesus delivered all verses in Matthew 5–7 at one time, the disciples' heads would have exploded." What do you think about this idea? Why might Matthew have collected many of Jesus's originally separate teachings into a single "sermon"?

The Beatitudes

Recruit a volunteer to read aloud Matthew 4:23–5:2. Ask:

- Why are large crowds following Jesus at this early point in his ministry?

- "It is no accident," writes AJ, "that the Sermon on the Mount is *on the mountain*." As she notes, mountains figure prominently in Matthew's Gospel. Read these texts in Matthew: 4:8-10; 14:22-23; 15:29-31; 17:1-6; 24:3; 28:16-20. What conclusions can you draw about what it means, for Matthew, for Jesus to be on a mountain? Have you ever had what might be called a "mountaintop experience"?

- AJ also writes "that mountain [in 5:1] should remind us of Mount Sinai, where Moses delivered the Torah to Israel." Read Exodus 19:1-8. Matthew and his original audience were, like Jesus and his first disciples, devout Jews, thoroughly familiar with the Scripture (what Christians call the Old Testament). How might remembering God's gift of the Torah (instruction; law) at Mount Sinai shape their expectations for Jesus's Sermon on the Mount?

- In her introduction, AJ notes that the term *sermon* initially did not encourage her to read the Sermon on the Mount. When you hear the term *sermon*, what do you expect to encounter?

- Also in her introduction, AJ recounts her long reluctance to read the Sermon on the Mount because Christians represented it to her as part of Jesus's supposed attempt to "fix Judaism." Only later did she learn that "Jesus is not a Christian talking to other Christians; he is a Jew talking to other Jews. He's not telling his fellow Jews to do away with Torah. . . . Rather, he's telling them that he has insight into the heart of Torah, and they would do well to listen to him." When, if ever, have you encountered the idea that the Sermon on the Mount corrects or contradicts Jewish observance of Torah? How can studying the Sermon as "a teaching given by one Jew to fellow Jews" contribute to improved relationships between Jews and Christians today?

Introducing the Beatitude Form

Recruit a volunteer to read aloud Matthew 5:3-12 while other participants read along silently. *Optional*: instruct the volunteer to pause after each of Jesus's sayings so other participants can read aloud any significant differences in the Bible version they are reading.

Explain, as AJ does, that some people call sayings of this type *makarisms* after the Greek New Testament word *makarioi*, often translated as "blessed." The word *beatitude* comes from Jerome's fourth-century translation of the Bible into Latin, in which this word is *beati*.

Point out that Jesus did not invent the beatitude form. Recruit volunteers to turn to and read aloud some or all of these verses: Genesis 14:18-20; Ruth 2:19-20; Psalm 84:4-5; Psalm 118:26; Proverbs 20:7; Jeremiah 17:7-8.

Ask:

- What do these beatitudes suggest about why and how someone is "blessed"?
- AJ lists several alternate ways of translating the statements the NRSV reads as "Blessed are"; these variants include "Happy are," "Fortunate are," and "Praiseworthy are." How else might you express the sentiment in biblical beatitudes (both Jesus's and others') in everyday language today?
- AJ writes, "When we hear that we are blessed, we should hear as well a sense of responsibility. A blessing given, a talent bestowed, if unappreciated and unused, is wasted." How, specifically, do you exercise responsibility as a response to the ways you consider yourself "blessed"?

Characterizing the Kingdom of Heaven

Remind participants that AJ presents the Sermon on the Mount as "a beginner's guide to the kingdom of heaven." She writes that, for Matthew, "Heaven is a different place, a better place, a real place, a place where God rules and life is as God wants rather than as humanity has constructed." Explain that Jesus's beatitudes introduce us to the contrast between life as the present world knows it and life as God wills it.

Have participants form small groups of a few people each. Assign each group one or two of the beatitudes, as total group size warrants. Ask each group to discuss these questions, which you will want to write on a markerboard, a large sheet of paper, or a prepared handout for ease of reference:

- Whom does this beatitude identify as "blessed" and for what reason?
- What does the Bible say about these "blessed" ones elsewhere? Can you remember or find specific Bible stories about individuals who belong to these categories? (Use Bible dictionaries and concordances, in print or online, to help you.)
- Based on this beatitude, what are God's priorities and how do they differ from human priorities? What is God's will for human life?
- What practical implications for how God's people should live do you draw from this beatitude?

After allowing sufficient time for small-group study, convene the whole group and invite each small group to talk about highlights from its discussion.

Expand discussion with some or all of these questions:

- Commenting on the first beatitude, AJ writes, "the poor in spirit are those who recognize that they are both the beneficiaries of the help of others and part of a system in which they are to pay it forward and help those whom they can." What do you think of this definition? Using this definition, would you describe yourself as "poor in spirit"? Why or why not? Can you name someone you know or have known whom you would call "poor in spirit"?
- "To be poor is not necessarily to be righteous," writes AJ. "Nor for the Gospels is being rich synonymous with being venal or evil."

How important is it to avoid "romanticizing poverty" or demonizing wealth, and how does the first beatitude help us do so?

- Reflecting on the second beatitude, AJ rejects the trite, inappropriate platitudes people often say to those who are grieving. She mentions the Jewish practice of "sitting shiva," the seven-day period in which mourners' friends and family comfort them "not by offering platitudes but by offering memory and story and presence." "To mourn in Israel," she writes, "means that we are not alone; we have not only our friends and relatives but also the previous generations and the generations to come. And we take comfort in that." When you have been in grief, what have been the most comforting words you have heard? What actions have made your grief more bearable? How does your congregation take the necessary time to comfort those who mourn?

- "In part," AJ notes, "those who mourn are blessed because not everyone can mourn. . . . A heart that knows how to grieve is a heart that knows how to love." Do you agree? Why or why not?

- Commenting on the third beatitude, AJ writes that "a meek person is a person with great authority, but one who does not lord it over others. A meek person promotes servant leadership over despotism." What "servant leaders" do you know or have you known? How has their example instructed or inspired you? Have you ever found yourself to be in a position of servant leadership?

- AJ suggests telling some people "to have a bit more humility is probably not the right advice." Instead, some people might do well to have a stronger sense of self. What situations do you know or can you think of in which her warning would apply?

- "Inheriting the earth, or the land," writes AJ, "is not a windfall; it is a responsibility." How does the third beatitude guide us to use the earth and its resources in righteous ways? Can you think of any resonances in the Sermon on the Mount where concern for the earth returns?

Optional Activity

Invite participants to look through recent newspapers and magazines for pictures and articles they believe could illustrate one or more of Jesus's beatitudes. Ask participants to present and explain their selections.

Closing Activity

Read aloud from *Sermon on the Mount*: "We can leave the Beatitudes with the phrase 'blessed are' ringing in our ears. We could attempt to recite all nine . . . but perhaps a better exercise is to continue the pattern and develop our own."

Distribute paper and pencils or pens to participants and encourage them to write their own beatitude expressing what, informed by this session's reading and discussion, they believe the kingdom of heaven is. After sufficient time, invite volunteers to read their new beatitudes aloud.

Pray this prayer or one in your own words:

> *Jesus our teacher, you are concerned not only with what we believe but also and especially with what we do. Send us out in your Spirit to practice righteousness, that we whom you graciously call "blessed" may live as blessings in the world, glorifying God in heaven. Amen.*

Session 2

THE EXTENSIONS

Session Goals

This session's reading, discussion, reflection, and prayer will equip participants to:

- Appreciate Jesus's reverence for the Torah.
- Understand how and why Jesus engaged in the rabbinic practice of "building a fence around Torah."
- Discuss each of Jesus's extensions in the Sermon on the Mount in its original context and its relevance for today.
- Recognize how Jesus's extensions nurture his ideal community.

Biblical Foundations

"Do not think that I have come to abolish the law or the prophets; I have come not to abolish but to fulfill. For truly I tell you, until heaven and earth pass away, not one letter, not one stroke of a letter, will pass from the law until all is accomplished. Therefore, whoever breaks one of the least of these commandments, and teaches others to do the same, will be called least in the kingdom of heaven; but whoever does them and teaches them will be called great in the kingdom of heaven. For I tell you, unless your righteousness exceeds that of the scribes and Pharisees, you will never enter the kingdom of heaven."

Matthew 5:17-20

11

Suggested Leader Preparation

- Carefully and prayerfully read Matthew 5:13-48; make notes of whatever grabs your attention most, sparks questions, or prompts new insights. If desired, consult a trusted Bible commentary.
- Carefully read chapter 2 of *Sermon on the Mount*. Note any material you need or want to research further before the session.
- Have on hand Bible dictionaries and concordances (or identify trusted online equivalents) and a variety of Bible translations for participants to use (recommended).
- If using the DVD or streaming video in your study, preview the session 2 segment and choose the best time in your session to view it.

As Your Group Gathers

Welcome participants. Ask those who attended the first session to talk briefly about what most interested, challenged, or helped them.

Ask volunteers to talk about how they understand the Torah. Do they find the various commandments to be burdensome, incomprehensible, antiquated, life-giving, or a combination. Ask them if they have ever studied the commandments or even just the famous "ten commandments."

Tell participants in this session that the group will explore how Jesus, like other ancient rabbis, is providing guidelines for living into the kingdom, for revealing how God wants us to live, by "building a fence around the Torah" in the second major section of the Sermon on the Mount.

Read aloud from *Sermon on the Mount*: "As a fence around a house protects what is inside, so the fence around the Torah protects the commandments by creating the circumstances that make violation more difficult."

Pray this prayer or one in your own words:

> *High and holy God, at Mount Sinai you graciously entrusted your chosen people, Israel, with the gift of your Torah; and on a*

hill in Galilee, your Son reaffirmed its gravity and its goodness. As we study his words today, may your Spirit again write your law on our hearts that we may live more faithfully as the holy community he and you call us to be. Amen.

Introducing the Extensions

Recruit a volunteer to read aloud Matthew 5:17-20. Ask:

- How would you describe Jesus's attitude toward God's Torah?
- What connection does Jesus make between observing Torah and the kingdom of heaven?
- "Jesus asserts," writes AJ, "that the Scripture of Israel remains sacred for his followers. . . . He never dismissed it; he never transgressed it." In your experience, to what extent do Christians share this regard for Torah?
- AJ also notes that, in some cases, Jesus and some of his contemporaries disagreed about how a commandment should be understood. Have you ever disagreed with the way others in your community have understood the Bible or church tradition?

Read the following aloud:

> Biblical scholars often call the teachings in this section of the Sermon the "antitheses" (opposites). AJ calls them extensions: "Jesus is not opposing Torah; he is extending it," teaching Torah's "core values."
>
> Like the Beatitudes, the extensions show how "Jesus is setting up an ideal community . . . where the group members replace the natal family's mother and brother and sisters. The group has only one father, the one who is in heaven."

Recruit volunteers to read each Scripture below aloud, then discuss each passage using the questions provided. (The questions often cite other Scriptures; you may read them as time allows, but, unless indicated, it is not essential you do so.)

First Extension: Building a Fence Around Murder

"You have heard that it was said to those of ancient times, 'You shall not murder'; and 'whoever murders shall be liable to judgment.' But I say to you that if you are angry with a brother or sister, you will be liable to judgment; and if you insult a brother or sister, you will be liable to the council; and if you say, 'You fool,' you will be liable to the hell of fire. So when you are offering your gift at the altar, if you remember that your brother or sister has something against you, leave your gift there before the altar and go; first be reconciled to your brother or sister, and then come and offer your gift. Come to terms quickly with your accuser while you are on the way to court with him, or your accuser may hand you over to the judge, and the judge to the guard, and you will be thrown into prison. Truly I tell you, you will never get out until you have paid the last penny."

Matthew 5:21-26

- Jesus quotes God's commandment against murder (Exodus 20:13; Deuteronomy 5:17) and likely paraphrases Genesis 9:6, which, like other Scripture (for example, Numbers 35:16-18), classifies murder as a capital offense. Other passages "undercut the idea of capital punishment," such as God protecting Cain (Genesis 4:13-15) and the example of Moses, who kills an Egyptian slave master (Exodus 2:11-15). AJ, who has worked with incarcerated men at a maximum-security prison, advises that when we recognize that people who commit murder "are also in the divine image, we need to come up with a response other than execution." How should Scripture shape our views on capital punishment?

- Tracing how Jewish concepts of the afterlife changed over time, AJ concludes that Jesus's "hell of fire" "is not eternal torture, but annihilation, or oblivion." (See Matthew 10:28.) How do you define hell? Does hell seem a just punishment for angry insults hurled at fellow believers (not to mention fellow members of the human family)? Explain.

- "Jesus sees connections between murder and insult, death and name-calling," AJ observes. "Names hurt. Names kill." How have you experienced—directly or indirectly, giving them or receiving them—the harmful power of names? When you hear people calling others hurtful names, how do you respond?

- AJ notes, "If we are not made angry by suffering, by cheating, by indifference, then we are not human." What examples of "righteous anger," if any, would you cite as exceptions to Jesus's extension? How do we discern whether our anger *is* righteous?

- This extension says we cannot properly worship God unless we are in proper relationship with other people (Matthew 5:23-24). When have your troubled relationships with others troubled your relationship with God? What did you do to improve these relationships? What happened?

- How does this extension help build Jesus's ideal community?

Second Extension: Building a Fence Around Adultery

"You have heard that it was said, 'You shall not commit adultery.' But I say to you that everyone who looks at a woman with lust has already committed adultery with her in his heart. If your right eye causes you to sin, tear it out and throw it away; it is better for you to lose one of your members than for your whole body to be thrown into hell. And if your right hand causes you to sin, cut it off and throw it away; it is better for you to lose one of your members than for your whole body to go into hell."

Matthew 5:27-30

- Jesus quotes God's prohibition of adultery (Exodus 20:14; Deuteronomy 5:18). AJ points out that in ancient Israel and in Jesus's time, *adultery* meant "sexual relations between a married or a betrothed woman and a man other than her husband or betrothed," but in those days "a Jewish man could have sexual relations with a divorcée, a prostitute, or an otherwise unmarried and unengaged woman." How does or should this historic double standard affect the way believers observe this command today?

- Leviticus 20:10 sentences both the man and woman who commit adultery to death, but AJ notes, "The rabbis generally sought to prevent the death penalty," including for adultery. Laws are always interpreted and reinterpreted. What laws, if any, can you think of, whether in church contexts or state contexts, that have been reinterpreted? What laws can you think of that *should* be reinterpreted?

- AJ suggests that Jesus's "fence" "does treat women as a commodity, as objects of desire," and she also observes that "Lust is not a sin reserved for heterosexual males." Do you agree? Why or why not? How does Jesus's "fence" speak to his society? What might he say to ours?

- How do Jesus's words in verses 29-30 influence your attitude toward the human body?

- How does this extension help build Jesus's ideal community?

Third Extension: Building a Fence Around Divorce

"It was also said, 'Whoever divorces his wife, let him give her a certificate of divorce.' But I say to you that anyone who divorces his wife, except on the ground of unchastity, causes her to commit adultery; and whoever marries a divorced woman commits adultery."

Matthew 5:31-32

- Jesus cites Deuteronomy 24:1-4, which, AJ explains, many ancient rabbis read as allowing "only adultery [as] grounds for divorce." But the words describing the grounds for breaking the marriage contract are "frustratingly vague" in both Deuteronomy and in Jesus's extension, and this vagueness has led to narrower and broader interpretations through history. How broad or narrow are your ideas about legitimate grounds for divorce? What about your religious community's views? Why do you hold the views you do?

- "Contrary to popular teaching," writes AJ, "Jesus's forbidding of divorce is not designed to protect women from husbands issuing arbitrary divorce decrees." Jewish women were protected financially by their marriage contracts. Moreover, in Mark's version of the divorce statement (Mark 10:12), Jesus forbids women from divorcing their husbands, and no one argues that he is protecting the husband's financial security. What, then, does Jesus want to accomplish with this extension?

- Read Matthew 19:3-9. How does Jesus's teaching about marriage in this text help illuminate his "fence" around divorce?

- "A marriage that looks like a battlefield is not a marriage sanctioned by God," writes AJ. "Not all marriages are made in heaven." How does or could your faith community help married people discern whether ending a marriage might be a more faithful course than continuing it? How does your faith community support those who are divorced?

- How does this extension help build Jesus's ideal community?

Fifth Extension: Building a Fence Against Violence

"You have heard that it was said, 'An eye for an eye and a tooth for a tooth.' But I say to you, Do not resist an evildoer. But if anyone strikes you on the right cheek, turn the other also; and if anyone wants to sue you and take your coat, give your cloak as well; and if anyone forces you to go one mile, go also the second mile. Give to everyone who begs from you, and do not refuse anyone who wants to borrow from you."

Matthew 5:38-42

- Jesus quotes Scriptures about compensation for bodily injuries (Exodus 21:22-25; Leviticus 24:19-20; Deuteronomy 19:15-21), designed to limit vengeful violence. AJ notes "we have no evidence that ancient Israelites or the Jews who came after" followed these laws, and "almost all rabbinic texts suggest that the formula must mean financial compensation." How have you heard the phrase "an eye for an eye" used in popular culture? How closely does this use conform to the facts of its origin?

- AJ states that Jesus "changes the subject" in this extension. How so, and for what purpose?
- How have you heard the phrase "turn the other cheek" used in popular culture? How closely does this use reflect Jesus's intent, as AJ explains it, to empower people who have been treated violently with a way of expressing "agency and courage"?
- What might a modern equivalent of "turning the other cheek" be—a nonviolent act by which those treated violently declare their refusal to be treated as less than human?
- How does this extension help build Jesus's ideal community?

Sixth Extension: Building a Fence Against Limiting Love

"You have heard that it was said, 'You shall love your neighbor and hate your enemy.' But I say to you, Love your enemies and pray for those who persecute you, so that you may be children of your Father in heaven; for he makes his sun rise on the evil and on the good, and sends rain on the righteous and on the unrighteous. For if you love those who love you, what reward do you have? Do not even the tax collectors do the same? And if you greet only your brothers and sisters, what more are you doing than others? Do not even the Gentiles do the same? Be perfect, therefore, as your heavenly Father is perfect."
Matthew 5:43-48

- Leviticus 19 commands Israelites to love their neighbor (verse 18) and "the alien" or stranger in the land (verse 34). How do these commands strengthen a community?
- Torah includes no command to "hate your enemy" but neither does it command the love of enemy, as Jesus commands

(although AJ notes that Proverbs 24:17 and Jeremiah 29:7 anticipate his instruction). Why does Jesus command his followers to love their enemies?

- AJ notes that keeping Jesus's command "first requires that we, in fact, love ourselves (a point that cannot be taken for granted)." How, specifically and practically, do we love ourselves in healthy and faithful ways? What factors make loving ourselves easier or more difficult?
- How are you praying for those you regard as enemies? Do you do more than pray for them, as Proverbs insists?
- Does loving an enemy mean ceasing to regard that person as an enemy? Why or why not?
- How does this extension help build Jesus's ideal community?

Optional Activity

In her book (because of space limitations), AJ does not discuss the fourth extension: Jesus's prohibition of oath-taking (5:33-36). If your group wishes to discuss it, ask:

- Jesus appears to be paraphrasing Torah's position on oaths rather than quoting a specific verse. What do Leviticus 19:11-12, Numbers 30:2, and Deuteronomy 23:21-23 teach about making and keeping oaths?
- How does Jesus extend the Torah's position on oaths?
- What oaths, if any, are you willing to make, and why? How valuable today is someone's oath or promise?
- How does this extension help build Jesus's ideal community?

Closing Activity

Read aloud again Matthew 5:17-20. Ask participants to define *righteousness* in their own words and to share how they see the extensions as related to righteousness.

Remind participants that Jesus's extensions address ethical threats to the life of his ideal community and offer proactive ways of mitigating those threats. Ask:

- What other ethical threats to Jesus's ideal community can you identify?
- What are some ways to mitigate those threats?

Pray this prayer or one in your own words:

> *Keep us vigilant, O God, against anything that seeks to destroy or diminish the fullness of life together for which you choose us. Keep us close to you and to our neighbors, and never so far from strangers and even enemies that we fail to extend love to them. Amen.*

Session 3

PRACTICING PIETY

Session Goals

This session's reading, discussion, reflection, and prayer will equip participants to:

- Appreciate Jesus's metaphorical descriptions of his disciples as salt and light.
- Articulate an accurate definition of *piety*, illustrated with personally meaningful examples.
- Understand why Jesus drew the contrasts he did between different types of almsgiving, prayer, and fasting.
- Form responses informed by Jesus's teaching to various attitudes about and exercises of piety.
- Reflect on how the ways they practice piety help them become complete and at peace both within themselves and in their relationships to others.

Biblical Foundations

"You are the salt of the earth; but if salt has lost its taste, how can its saltiness be restored? It is no longer good for anything, but is thrown out and trampled under foot.

"You are the light of the world. A city built on a hill cannot be hid. No one after lighting a lamp puts it under the bushel

basket, but on the lampstand, and it gives light to all in the house. In the same way, let your light shine before others, so that they may see your good works and give glory to your Father in heaven."

Matthew 5:13-16

"Beware of practicing your piety before others in order to be seen by them; for then you have no reward from your Father in heaven.

"So whenever you give alms, do not sound a trumpet before you, as the hypocrites do in the synagogues and in the streets, so that they may be praised by others. Truly I tell you, they have received their reward. But when you give alms, do not let your left hand know what your right hand is doing, so that your alms may be done in secret; and your Father who sees in secret will reward you.

"And whenever you pray, do not be like the hypocrites; for they love to stand and pray in the synagogues and at the street corners, so that they may be seen by others. Truly I tell you, they have received their reward. But whenever you pray, go into your room and shut the door and pray to your Father who is in secret; and your Father who sees in secret will reward you.

"When you are praying, do not heap up empty phrases as the Gentiles do; for they think that they will be heard because of their many words. Do not be like them, for your Father knows what you need before you ask him. . . .

"And whenever you fast, do not look dismal, like the hypocrites, for they disfigure their faces so as to show others that they are fasting. Truly I tell you, they have received their reward. But when you fast, put oil on your head and wash your face, so that your fasting may be seen not by others but by your Father who is in secret; and your Father who sees in secret will reward you."

Matthew 6:1-8, 16-18

Suggested Leader Preparation

- Carefully and prayerfully read these passages and make notes of whatever grabs your attention most and sparks questions or new insights. If desired, consult a trusted Bible commentary.
- Carefully read chapter 3 of *Sermon on the Mount*. Note any material you need or want to research further before the session.
- Have on hand a variety of Bible translations and trusted study Bibles and commentaries for participants to use (recommended) and newspapers and magazines (optional). You will also need a salty snack to share (saltines, salted pretzels, salted nuts—have alternatives for participants with food allergies) and a wax or electric candle placed where all participants may see it.
- If using the DVD or streaming video in your study, preview the session 3 segment and choose the best time in your session to view it.

As Your Group Gathers

Welcome participants. Ask those who attended the previous session to talk briefly about what most interested, challenged, or helped them.

Light the candle and distribute the salty snack to participants. As the group eats, ask them to name as many qualities or properties of light and salt as they can. Write responses on a large sheet of paper or markerboard.

Read aloud Matthew 5:13-16. Ask:

- Why does Jesus call his disciples "the salt of the earth"?
- Why does Jesus call his disciples "the light of the world"?
- How are these two metaphors alike and unalike? Which one, if either, do you more identify with, and why?
- If you could add another metaphor to "salt of the earth" and "light of the world" to describe the actions of your faith community, what would it be, and why?

Tell participants that Jesus uses metaphors of salt and light for his followers because, like both salt and light, his disciples "are valuable not simply because of who they are but also and especially for what they contribute to the world."

Ask participants:

- How do you define *piety*?
- Does the idea of piety sound positive or negative to you? Why?

After acknowledging responses, share AJ's definition of piety: "our expressions of our religious commitments." Read aloud from *Sermon on the Mount*: "To be a disciple means less about believing in a set of propositions and more about acting upon God's Word as interpreted by Jesus." This session will explore how Jesus instructs his disciples in how properly to practice piety.

Pray this prayer or one in your own words:

> *Holy God, you who graciously shines your goodness on the world: May your Spirit guide us, in this time together, toward greater understanding of how what we believe must shape what we do, that we may increasingly glorify you before others, in the name of our Teacher and Savior, Jesus Christ. Amen.*

If using a lit wax candle, extinguish it now.

Studies in Contrast

Read aloud Matthew 6:1. Ask:

- How, if at all, do you believe God rewards those who practice piety?
- How do we understand Jesus's admonition to avoid practicing piety before others when he also describes his followers as those who "let [their] light shine before others" (5:16)?
- Tell participants that the Greek word the NRSV translates as "piety" in Matthew 6 is the same word (*dikaiosynē*) usually translated as "righteousness" or "justice." Ask them how they understand the relationship of piety to righteousness.

Read aloud from *Sermon on the Mount*: "To be righteous, to practice the correct type of piety, is to have one foot in the kingdom of heaven. . . . Jesus is looking not only at the action but also at the motive behind it."

Form three teams of participants. Assign each group one of the three "studies in contrast" Jesus speaks about in this section of the Sermon:

- contrasting ways of giving alms (6:2-4)
- contrasting ways of praying (6:5-8; tell participants that session 4 will cover the Lord's Prayer)
- contrasting ways of fasting (6:16-18)

Ask each team to discuss this question: "How does this 'study in contrast' illustrate Jesus's teachings about true piety?"

After allowing sufficient time for discussion, reconvene the whole group and have a spokesperson from each team talk about highlights from the team's discussion. Encourage teams to consult both AJ's book as well as study Bibles and commentaries as desired.

After all teams have reported, continue and expand the discussion using some or all of these questions:

Almsgiving

- "Folks in the first century were not walking around with a trumpet," writes AJ, "or a shofar (a ram's horn) or a saxophone and tooting every time someone donated a shekel." What does Jesus mean, then, when he tells his disciples not to "sound a trumpet" when they give money?
- How do some gift givers in our society today "sound a trumpet" when they give?
- Read or review AJ's summary of the twelfth-century Jewish philosopher Maimonides's eight levels of charity. At what level is most of your giving? If you are dissatisfied with your usual level of giving, what steps will you take to change it?
- What do you see to be the advantages and disadvantages of announcing how much time or money someone has donated to a good cause?

Praying

- Jesus criticizes two kinds of praying, explains AJ: prayer that is "showing off" (the word *hypocrite* in verse 5 derives from an ancient Greek term for acting on stage) and prayer that attempts to manipulate God. Can you remember (and, if so, are you willing to talk about) times when you have strayed to one or the other (or both) of these kinds of prayers? How might you guard against hypocrisy or manipulative praying?

- "All conversations with God are a form of prayer," writes AJ. How would you characterize most of your conversations with God?

- "Prayer in anger is *not* hypocrisy; it is honesty," suggests AJ. How often, if ever, are you angry with God in your prayers? If you have been angry with God in prayer, how have you felt about your relationship with God afterward?

- AJ tells a story about a boy who went to the synagogue and prayed aloud the first three letters of the Hebrew alphabet. When the rabbi asked what he was doing, he said, "I don't know the prayers and I can't read, but if I just say the letters, God puts the prayer together for me." When have you trusted God to "put your prayer together for you"? (Compare Psalm 139:1-4; Romans 8:26-27).

- AJ suggests we can use the Psalms to prompt us when we don't feel we know how to pray. Which Psalms, if any, have you used in this way? How has praying with the Psalms affected your conversations with God?

- The Jewish tradition takes a lesson from the prayer of Hannah (1 Samuel 1:13), AJ explains, such that people form the words of the set prayers on their lips "no matter if we know the prayer by heart" because "prayer is a matter not only of the heart but also of the body." Further, reciting the words with our lips keeps us from speeding through the prayer. What bodily actions, if any, does your congregation use when praying? How do you personally use your body when you pray? What other ways could you try? How is an embodied prayer different from one only prayed with the voice or in silence?

Fasting

- What experience have you had with fasting as a religious practice? What difference does it make, if any, whether you fast as part of a community initiative or you fast on your own?
- What does Jesus's instruction about fasting have in common with his instruction about prayer?
- How do you understand fasting in light of famine and food insecurity? How is it different from dieting? Does fasting remind you of privilege or poverty? Does it put you more in touch with your body?

Optional Activity

1. If your group contains any would-be thespians, or at least adults who are willing to have some fun while studying Scripture, challenge each of the three teams to plan and perform a brief skit dramatizing their assigned "study in contrast."
2. Challenge each team to illustrate its assigned "study in contrast" with pictures from newspapers and magazines. Combine everyone's pictures into a collage and display in your church building or online for the rest of the congregation to view.
3. Play a game of "Piety Pictionary." On a large sheet of paper or markerboard, volunteers sketch pictures of activities they believe meet Jesus's criteria for true piety. The player who first guesses the activity being drawn is the next to draw.

Closing Activity

Invite participants to respond to each of the following statements based on what they have read and discussed during this session about Jesus's instructions regarding piety:

- I only give to charities when I can be sure I'll get a receipt for my taxes.
- I don't claim a tax deduction for my charitable giving because Jesus commanded us to give in secret.
- I won't pray aloud in public because Jesus told us to pray in private.
- I don't think we should use prewritten prayers in worship because true prayer is spontaneous and from the heart.
- I don't receive ashes on Ash Wednesday because Jesus told us not to disfigure our faces when we fast.

After discussing participants' responses, read aloud from *Sermon on the Mount*: "If [a pious] practice is based in justice, that's fine; if it's based on self-interest, 'in order to be seen by' others, then it's not. . . . When motive and action work in harmony, when the head is aligned with the heart, then we are moving toward that goal of 'completion' or 'perfection.'" Read aloud Matthew 5:48: "Be perfect, therefore, as your heavenly Father is perfect." Explain that "perfection," for Jesus, is not, as AJ writes, "a type of perfectionism that would necessarily make us all neurotic" but a process of becoming the people God created us to be, "complete and at peace." Ask:

- How do the ways you practice piety help you feel complete and at peace within yourself?
- How do the ways you practice piety find completion and peace in reaching out to and working toward justice for others?

After a short time for silent reflection, invite volunteers to talk about their responses. Be ready to offer a response of your own.

Pray this prayer or one in your own words:

Agitate us, O Spirit of God! Stir us so we dare not rest content with faith that leads to complacency and self-satisfaction. Drive us to give, pray, fast, and take other actions that make us more complete by showing love to and compassion for others and by bringing glory to you. Amen.

Session 4

OUR FATHER

Session Goals

This session's reading, discussion, reflection, and prayer will equip participants to:

- Discuss meaningful experiences of praying the Lord's Prayer.
- Think about and articulate multiple purposes of prayer.
- Examine each petition of the Lord's Prayer in light of Jesus's Jewish tradition.
- Think and speak about ways each petition in the Lord's Prayer connects with individual and communal experience.
- Commit to the spiritual discipline of praying the Lord's Prayer at least once a day for a limited time.

Biblical Foundations

"Pray then in this way:

> *Our Father in heaven,*
>> *hallowed be your name.*
>> *Your kingdom come.*
>> *Your will be done,*
>>> *on earth as it is in heaven.*
>> *Give us this day our daily bread.*
>> *And forgive us our debts,*

as we also have forgiven our debtors.
And do not bring us to the time of trial,
but rescue us from the evil one.

For if you forgive others their trespasses, your heavenly Father
will also forgive you; but if you do not forgive others, neither
will your Father forgive your trespasses."

Matthew 6:9-15

Hear, O Israel: The LORD is our God, the LORD alone. You
shall love the LORD your God with all your heart, and with
all your soul, and with all your might. Keep these words that I
am commanding you today in your heart. Recite them to your
children and talk about them when you are at home and when
you are away, when you lie down and when you rise. Bind
them as a sign on your hand, fix them as an emblem on your
forehead, and write them on the doorposts of your house and
on your gates.

Deuteronomy 6:4-9

Suggested Leader Preparation

- Carefully and prayerfully read Matthew 6:9-15, making notes of whatever grabs your attention most, sparks new questions, or prompts new insights. If desired, consult a trusted Bible commentary.

- Carefully read chapter 4 of *Sermon on the Mount*. Note any material you need or want to research further before the session.

- Have on hand a variety of Bible translations and trusted study Bibles and commentaries for participants to use (recommended). You will need at least two different translations of Matthew 6:9-13.

- If using the DVD or streaming video in your study, preview the session 4 segment and choose the best time in your session to view it.

As Your Group Gathers

Welcome participants. Ask those who attended the previous session to talk briefly about what most interested, challenged, or helped them.

Ask:

- What is your earliest memory of prayer?
- If you can recite the Lord's Prayer by heart, do you remember when and how you first learned it?
- Do you recall hearing different versions of the Lord's Prayer? What were they?
- When, if ever, have you found the Lord's Prayer particularly meaningful? Why?
- Do you recite any other prayers by heart? When and why?

Tell participants that this session invites us to explore the Lord's Prayer from a perspective with which most Christians are unfamiliar: "a prayer one Jew teaches his fellow Jews," in AJ's words. By examining Jesus's prayer in as much of its original context as we can recover, we may find it becomes even more meaningful.

Pray this prayer or one in your own words:

Holy God, Jesus taught us to pray to you with openness, expectation, and love. As we study the example he gave us, may we grow in faithfulness to you, led by your Spirit always to trust your faithfulness to us. Amen.

The Purposes of Prayer

Ask: "What do you believe is the purpose of prayer?" Acknowledge responses and write them down on a large sheet of paper or markerboard.

Summarize the five purposes of prayer that AJ discusses in chapter 4:

1. Prayer "allows us to express, honestly, our feelings" to God.
2. Prayer nurtures our connection to God: "The more we pray, the better we can develop our relationship with the divine."

3. Prayer is a way of "uniting ourselves to our communities and to our past."
4. Prayer in community "reminds us we are not all in the same" life circumstances.
5. Prayer "is particularly helpful for matters of discernment."

Ask:

- Of the purposes AJ discusses, which do you consider more important to you personally, and why?
- Which of these purposes, if any, do you find difficult to accept, and why?
- AJ states that her list of prayer's purposes is not exhaustive. What, if anything, would you add to it, and why?

The Lord's Prayer Line by Line

Recruit two or three volunteers to read Matthew 6:9-13 aloud in different translations. Ask participants to note how the translations differ from one another and how they may differ from the text your congregation recites in worship. Encourage participants to be alert for reasons behind these differences as you study the text.

Lead a line-by-line discussion of the text, using some or all of these questions:

Matthew 6:9a

- AJ demonstrates that Jesus was not novel or unique in calling God "Father": "Hardly blasphemous, *abba* [Father, not 'daddy' as in modern Hebrew] was a term other Jews used to address God. . . . To call God 'Father' is to evoke all the positive images of paternity." What are these positive images? What other names or images, if any, could people who are uncomfortable or upset by calling God "Father" use and still claim the close, positive relationship with God that Jesus experienced and wanted his followers to share?

- Citing Malachi 2:10, AJ notes "claiming God as our Father has ethical implications." What are these implications? How do you live them out?

- "For Jesus and his followers," writes AJ, "God is the only 'father'" (see Matthew 23:9). How does claiming only God as Father reshape our relationships to our human families? How are we to act when our relationships with God and our human families conflict?

- AJ notes, "When the followers of Jesus talked about their Father in the heavens, they were making a political statement," because Caesar claimed the title "father of the fatherland" for himself. How does claiming God as our Father make us reconsider our relationship to earthly authorities? How are we to act when these relationships come into conflict?

Matthew 6:9b

- Jesus prays that God's name will be "hallowed" (sanctified; made holy; "exalted and glorified"), a dominant theme in Jewish liturgy and prayer. "We still have to ask," writes AJ, "*who* is doing the hallowing?" How do you understand Jesus's petition? How does God make God's name holy? Can human beings make God's name holy and, if so, how?

- AJ notes that the name of God revealed to Moses is, in Hebrew, *eheyeh asher eheyeh*, "I will be what I will be." "The Hebrew testifies to divine freedom. God will be whatever God will be. . . . No theological determination or personal theology can box God in." What does the idea of God's freedom mean to you? If God is supremely free to be whatever God will be, what can we say with certainty about God?

- According to AJ, "This freedom also means that God can be part of a conversation." How much would you say your prayers are conversations with God? How can we discern when our conversations with God are becoming one-sided—our side only?

- Contrasting God's name in Exodus with Jesus's "I Am" statements in John's Gospel, AJ states, "Greek thought preferred the permanent, the unchanging; Hebrew thought preferred the open possibility." She asks, "What kind of God should we proclaim [today]?" How would you answer her question, and why? What are the ethical implications of proclaiming either an unchanging and impassive God or a God of open possibility and emotions? How do you prefer to think of God, and why?

Matthew 6:10

- "We should take 'kingdom' language seriously," writes AJ, "because [Jesus], not we, lived in a kingdom, without democracy, ruled by an emperor and maintained by an army." How does considering his status as a Jew living in Galilee, ruled by a puppet of Rome, and visiting occupied Judea ruled by a Roman governor shape how you understand for what Jesus is praying with the words "your kingdom come"? How might his understanding and that of his first disciples compare with what you are praying for when you pray this portion of the Lord's Prayer?

- Should Christians who live in a modern democracy search for language and images other than "kingdom" to describe what Jesus is praying for? If not, why not? If so, what might these other possibilities be?

- According to AJ, "America's famous 'separation of church and state' does not mean that churches should be silent in the face of oppression." How do churches know when making a political protest, as AJ suggests this petition in the Lord's Prayer does, is appropriate and necessary? What forms besides prayer, if any, should such protests take? What forms have they taken throughout American religious history, and do you find these examples appropriate?

- AJ writes, "To determine divine will, such that we can enact it ourselves, . . . we study the word of God and then engage with others on how to understand it." How important is group study of Scripture (distinct from hearing Scripture read and interpreted in worship) in your congregation? When, specifically and practically, has studying Scripture in a community helped you discern and carry out God's will?

- AJ notes that Jesus, like several people in Israel's Scriptures, demonstrates that "sometimes, divine will is not what we will." (See Matthew 26:39.) When was a time you discovered that God's will and your will did not align? How did you respond? What happened?

Matthew 6:11

- According to AJ, the Greek term usually translated "daily" is probably better understood to mean "for tomorrow" or "for the future." Read Isaiah 25:6 and 25:9, which AJ cites as one ancient Jewish connection of food with the "world to come." How does this prophecy shape your understanding of what Jesus is praying for when praying for "tomorrow's bread"?
- Read Exodus 16:13-21, a portion of the story of God feeding the Israelites with manna in the wilderness. How does this story inform the way we pray for bread? What should a people who pray for each day's bread do and not do with their food? What changes, if any, would you need to make in your personal use of food to meet these expectations?
- "At the synagogue," explains AJ, "after we welcome the Sabbath, we serve food. Why? Because the Sabbath is a foretaste—literally—of the world to come. For the church, the Communion or Eucharist is part of this celebration." How much do your congregation's observances of Holy Communion (the Lord's Supper) seem like celebrations of God's future world? How does or how might your congregation make this aspect of Communion clear?

Matthew 6:12

- "'Sin' in Hebrew thought has actual content—it is a 'thing'—and so metaphors were needed to understand it," one of which is the metaphor of "debt" that Jesus uses in the Lord's Prayer. AJ explains the metaphor this way: "as if we all had heavenly bank accounts, and when we sinned, the account became drained. Forgiveness restores the balance." How helpful do you find this metaphor for sin and forgiveness? With what other metaphors for sin are you familiar?

- AJ explains that forgiveness "restores the balance . . . between humanity and divinity as well as among members of a community." How do verses 14-15 make the connection between divine and human forgiveness clear? How do you react to the idea of God forgiving us only as we forgive others?
- AJ suggests that the "debts" language in Matthew's version of the Lord's Prayer (contrast Luke 11:4) means "Jesus's followers remembered that he was concerned not only about forgiving sins . . . but also about economic justice." How and how much do you think churches should address economic justice? Why?
- In calling his disciples to forgive people, writes AJ, "Jesus is not calling people to be doormats." How can we forgive those who sin against us without inviting or encouraging them to do so again?

Matthew 6:13

- AJ explains that the Greek noun in this petition can be translated as "temptation," "test," or "trial" with equal accuracy. How does each translation affect how you understand what Jesus is praying for?
- Acknowledging James 1:13-14, AJ states, "And yet Scripture does tell us that God tests us," with God's test of Abraham in Genesis 22 as one instance. Do you believe God tests people? Why or why not? How, if at all, do you believe God has tested or is testing you?
- "At the same time," AJ writes, "God gives us the resources to overcome temptation." When, if ever, have you experienced God strengthening you to overcome temptation? What happened?
- Rabbinic tradition, explains AJ, came to think of Satan less as a

malevolent counterforce to God and more as he is in the book of Job: "a being in the heavenly court who tests people, usually righteous people; he is also usually defeated, and his defeat demonstrates the righteousness of the person tested." Do you believe an "evil one" exists? Why or why not? If not, what do you believe about the presence of evil in the world and God's relationship to evil?

- AJ observes, "Good Jewish teacher that he is, Jesus doesn't ask of his disciples anything he does not already ask of himself." How does Jesus model a faithful response to being tempted or tested by "the evil one" in Matthew 4:1-11?

Optional Activity

Listen together to several musical settings of the Lord's Prayer, especially contrasting versions and settings in different languages. (A quick internet search will yield plenty of choices.)

Ask:

- Which of these musical settings most appeals to you and why?
- How does this activity give you new insights into the Lord's Prayer?

Closing Activity

Invite a volunteer to read aloud Deuteronomy 6:4-9. Read aloud from *Sermon on the Mount*: "For some, prayer is as much a part of the daily routine as brushing one's teeth (both are healthy activities)."

Ask:

- How much is prayer a part of your day at home and away, when you lie down and when you rise up?
- How will or how could you incorporate the Lord's Prayer into your daily living—or incorporate it even more than you do now?

Challenge participants to commit to praying the Lord's Prayer at least once a day before the next session, and even to take brief notes about any changes they experience to which this discipline could contribute. Emphasize that you are asking participants to treat the Lord's Prayer not as magic but as a resource for strengthening their relationship to God and to their community.

Close this session by praying together the version of the Lord's Prayer with which your congregation is most familiar.

Session 5

FINDING YOUR TREASURE

Session Goals

This session's reading, discussion, reflection, and prayer will equip participants to:

- Reflect on what they associate with and how they connect the ideas of treasure, wealth, and stuff.
- Explore and talk about five ways Jesus, in the Sermon on the Mount, instructs his disciples to seek true treasure: faithful fasting, serving God rather than mammon, taking care for what they see (physically and spiritually), avoiding worry, and avoiding judgmentalism.
- Imagine situations in the news and in daily life that would be changed for the better if people committed themselves to Jesus's ways of seeking true treasure.

Biblical Foundations

"Do not store up for yourselves treasures on earth, where moth and rust consume and where thieves break in and steal; but store up for yourselves treasures in heaven, where neither moth nor rust consumes and where thieves do not break in and steal. For where your treasure is, there your heart will be also.

"The eye is the lamp of the body. So, if your eye is healthy, your whole body will be full of light; but if your eye is unhealthy,

your whole body will be full of darkness. If then the light in you is darkness, how great is the darkness!

"No one can serve two masters; for a slave will either hate the one and love the other, or be devoted to the one and despise the other. You cannot serve God and wealth.

"Therefore I tell you, do not worry about your life, what you will eat or what you will drink, or about your body, what you will wear. Is not life more than food, and the body more than clothing? Look at the birds of the air; they neither sow nor reap nor gather into barns, and yet your heavenly Father feeds them. Are you not of more value than they? And can any of you by worrying add a single hour to your span of life? And why do you worry about clothing? Consider the lilies of the field, how they grow; they neither toil nor spin, yet I tell you, even Solomon in all his glory was not clothed like one of these. But if God so clothes the grass of the field, which is alive today and tomorrow is thrown into the oven, will he not much more clothe you—you of little faith? Therefore do not worry, saying, 'What will we eat?' or 'What will we drink?' or 'What will we wear?' For it is the Gentiles who strive for all these things; and indeed your heavenly Father knows that you need all these things. But strive first for the kingdom of God and his righteousness, and all these things will be given to you as well.

"So do not worry about tomorrow, for tomorrow will bring worries of its own. Today's trouble is enough for today.

"Do not judge, so that you may not be judged. For with the judgment you make you will be judged, and the measure you give will be the measure you get. Why do you see the speck in your neighbor's eye, but do not notice the log in your own eye? Or how can you say to your neighbor, 'Let me take the speck out of your eye,' while the log is in your own eye? You hypocrite, first take the log out of your own eye, and then you will see clearly to take the speck out of your neighbor's eye."

Matthew 6:19–7:5

Suggested Leader Preparation

- Carefully and prayerfully read Matthew 6:19–7:5, making notes of whatever grabs your attention most, sparks new questions, or prompts new insights. If desired, consult a trusted Bible commentary.
- Carefully read chapter 5 from *Sermon on the Mount*. Note any material you need or want to research further before the session.
- Have on hand a variety of Bible translations and trusted study Bibles and commentaries for participants to use (recommended). You will also need recent newspapers and magazines.
- If using the DVD or streaming video in your study, preview the session 5 segment and choose the best time in your session to view it.

As Your Group Gathers

Welcome participants. Ask those who attended the previous session to talk briefly about what most interested, challenged, or helped them.

Ask participants to free associate in response to the three words listed below. Encourage participants to think quickly and to avoid censoring or judging their responses. Write down responses in lists on a large sheet of paper or markerboard.

- wealth
- treasure
- stuff

Invite participants to review the lists of responses. Ask:

- What observations can you make about our responses?
- What relationships, if any, do you see among "wealth," "treasure," and "stuff"?

Tell participants that this session explores Jesus's teachings on wealth, treasure, and stuff as presented in the Sermon on the Mount.

These teachings, as AJ explains in *Sermon on the Mount*, help Jesus's followers "recognize priorities" and "find the treasure that awaits."

Pray this prayer or one of your own:

> *Bountiful and generous God, we thank you for giving us this time together to read and reflect on Jesus's teachings. May your Spirit help us treasure his word so that we may grow richer in faith toward you and in love toward others. Amen.*

Five Ways to Find True Treasure

Using the questions below, guide your group in a discussion of how Jesus teaches his disciples to find true treasure. If you have a large group, consider forming smaller teams and assigning each team one of the five topics below to discuss.

1. Faithful Fasting

Recruit a volunteer to read aloud Matthew 6:16-18.

Remind participants that they read and discussed Jesus's instructions on fasting (Matthew 6:16-18) in session 3, where they focused on the admonition against piety practiced for show. Tell them that AJ discusses the verses here as part of the Sermon on the Mount's guidance on finding treasure.

Ask:

- AJ suggests several ways in which fasting can help us find true treasure. It can be a way to appreciate what we have, to exercise self-control, to experience community, to show solidarity with those who are hungry, and to protest injustice. Have you ever experienced these dimensions of fasting? What other healthy aspects of fasting, if any, would you add to AJ's list?
- AJ mentions the Jewish fast day of Yom Kippur (the Day of Atonement) and the Islamic daily fast during the month of Ramadan. Among Christians, fasting sometimes occurs during Lent, the penitential season of preparation for Easter. Why do

many Christian traditions consider fasting an appropriate way to prepare for Easter? Do you observe a Lenten fast? If so, how has it helped you find true treasure?

- "Pastors and Bible study leaders would do well," writes AJ, "to use these verses as prompts to speak about anorexia and bulimia, to show the difference between healthy and unhealthy fasting, and to point out to friends and families the warning signs of eating disorders." What are the differences between healthy and unhealthy fasting? Have eating disorders affected you or someone you know? How can the church do a better job helping people who struggle with food?

2. Mastering Mammon

Recruit a volunteer to read aloud Matthew 6:19-21 and 6:24. Ask:

- "'Treasure on earth' is, in this context, just what it sounds like," writes AJ. Jesus "is talking about stuff, stuff that can be destroyed by human and natural forces." Talk about a time in which you have experienced the loss of stuff that mattered to you. How did that loss affect you?
- Talk about a time you have experienced stuff's power to pull at your heart (v. 21).
- What does it mean, practically speaking, to "store up . . . treasures in heaven" (v. 20)? Is Jesus's teaching here in tension with the Christian teaching of salvation by grace through faith? Why or why not?
- AJ critiques the translation of the Aramaic word *mammon* in verse 24 as "wealth" (NRSV), preferring, as did Matthew, to leave it untranslated: "To Greek speakers (and perhaps to English speakers today), setting God in opposition to mammon—an unfamiliar term—makes mammon, or all of our *stuff*, sound more like another god or idol." How do you see the opposition of God and mammon in society today? in your community? in your congregation? in your own life?

- AJ says the encounter between Jesus and a rich young man "reads like a gloss on [this] passage in the Sermon on the Mount." Read the story in Matthew 19:16-22. Why is it that, in AJ's words, "those who store up treasures on earth," as the rich young man did, "will have proportionally fewer treasures in heaven"?

3. The Lamp of the Body

Recruit a volunteer to read aloud Matthew 6:22-23. Ask:

- AJ quotes the ancient Roman orator Cicero: "The face is a picture of the mind as the eyes are its interpreter." What do you believe you can tell about someone by looking them in the eyes? Why?
- AJ explains that "in antiquity, many people thought that the eye projected light out, hence the connection between eyes and lamps." Given this background, how would you paraphrase Jesus's teaching in these verses in language a modern audience would understand?
- Although Jesus spoke of the eye projecting light outward, what might these verses teach us about what we "take in" by looking? How might that determine where we find treasure—and if we find true treasure?

4. Do Not Worry

Recruit one volunteer to read aloud Matthew 6:25-30, and another to read aloud 6:31-35. Ask:

- What is the most important thing you have worried about in the past week? The least important? What helps you feel better when you are feeling worried?
- In 1988, singer Bobby McFerrin recorded a (tongue-in-cheek) song whose refrain became almost a mantra: "Don't worry; be happy." What, if anything, makes Jesus's teaching in these verses a different message?

- AJ notes that Jesus is using "idealized" images. Can observing "the birds of the air" (v. 26) and "the lilies of the field" (v. 28) lead to contradictory conclusions about God's care? How do we learn to look at the natural world in the way Jesus looked at it?
- "Jesus is not saying we should be like the birds or the lilies," AJ points out. How do we work in the present and plan for the future without succumbing to worry and fear?
- When are you most aware of the "simplicity" and "ephemeral-ity" of life, and how does this awareness shape where you find treasure?
- Read James 2:1-4, which AJ cites in connection to these verses. What ethical implications for how we treat others does James draw from Jesus's teaching about a refusal to worry over food and clothing?
- What ethical implications do these verses in the Sermon carry for how we view and use the natural world?

5. Do Not Judge

Recruit a volunteer to read aloud Matthew 7:1-5. Ask:

- Why do human beings have a hard time not judging each other?
- In what area of life are you most likely to judge others, and why? In what are of life are others most likely to judge you?
- Why does Jesus tell his followers to refrain from judging others? How do you respond to this rationale?
- Jesus "is not saying that we should become bystanders," AJ explains, "or that we should not seek justice." How is judging different from being judgmental? How do we discern when we have trespassed from the former to the latter?
- Read Romans 14:1-12, which AJ cites in discussing these verses. What rationale does Paul give for refusing to judge others? How is it like or unlike Jesus's rationale?
- AJ describes how these verses in the Sermon made a new impact on her when teaching students at a maximum-security

prison: "As if they were channeling Jesus, they ask, 'Would you want to be judged by, or even known by, the worst thing you've ever done in your life?'" How would remembering this question reshape the way you think about other people?

- How does refusing to judge others help us find true treasure?

Closing Activity

Read aloud from *Sermon on the Mount*: Jesus sets "a high bar, just as Torah sets a high bar" for life in the kingdom of heaven.

Ask: "Which of the five ways of finding true treasure we discussed in this session seems the highest bar to you, and why?" Be ready to encourage discussion with your own response.

Distribute newspapers and magazines. Instruct participants, by taking their cues from this session's readings and discussion, to find a news item they think illustrates a failure to discover true treasure. Encourage them briefly to rewrite or summarize the news item as it would read had the people involved put Jesus's teaching on finding true treasure into practice. (Alternatively, you could invite participants similarly to revise such a situation from their own experience.)

Read aloud from *Sermon on the Mount*: "It's a process, but like muscle memory, living into the kingdom does become easier with intention and practice."

Ask: "What specific ways will you practice 'living into the kingdom' before our next and final session?"

Pray this prayer or one of your own:

> *Holy Spirit, ever guide us and strengthen us to seek first the kingdom of heaven and God's righteousness so that we may receive from God's open hands all true treasure as well, for the sake of Jesus our Teacher and Lord. Amen.*

Session 6

LIVING INTO THE KINGDOM

Session Goals

This session's reading, discussion, reflection, and prayer will equip participants to:

- Articulate their understanding of Jesus's description of the "narrow gate" and road leading to life in the kingdom of heaven.
- Identify the challenges to living as Jesus's ideal community discussed in the conclusion of the Sermon on the Mount.
- Reflect on how this study of the Sermon on the Mount has influenced their understandings of themselves, of the faith community, and of God.

Biblical Foundations

"Do not give what is holy to dogs; and do not throw your pearls before swine, or they will trample them under foot and turn and maul you.

"Ask, and it will be given you; search, and you will find; knock, and the door will be opened for you. For everyone who asks receives, and everyone who searches finds, and for everyone who knocks, the door will be opened. Is there anyone among you who, if your child asks for bread, will give a stone? Or if the child asks for a fish, will give a snake? If you then,

who are evil, know how to give good gifts to your children, how much more will your Father in heaven give good things to those who ask him!

"In everything do to others as you would have them do to you; for this is the law and the prophets.

"Enter through the narrow gate; for the gate is wide and the road is easy that leads to destruction, and there are many who take it. For the gate is narrow and the road is hard that leads to life, and there are few who find it.

"Beware of false prophets, who come to you in sheep's clothing but inwardly are ravenous wolves. You will know them by their fruits. Are grapes gathered from thorns, or figs from thistles? In the same way, every good tree bears good fruit, but the bad tree bears bad fruit. A good tree cannot bear bad fruit, nor can a bad tree bear good fruit. Every tree that does not bear good fruit is cut down and thrown into the fire. Thus you will know them by their fruits.

"Not everyone who says to me, 'Lord, Lord,' will enter the kingdom of heaven, but only the one who does the will of my Father in heaven. On that day many will say to me, 'Lord, Lord, did we not prophesy in your name, and cast out demons in your name, and do many deeds of power in your name?' Then I will declare to them, 'I never knew you; go away from me, you evildoers.'

"Everyone then who hears these words of mine and acts on them will be like a wise man who built his house on rock. The rain fell, the floods came, and the winds blew and beat on that house, but it did not fall, because it had been founded on rock. And everyone who hears these words of mine and does not act on them will be like a foolish man who built his house on sand. The rain fell, and the floods came, and the winds blew and beat against that house, and it fell—and great was its fall!"

Matthew 7:6-27

Suggested Leader Preparation

- Carefully and prayerfully read Matthew 7:6-27, making notes of whatever grabs your attention, sparks new questions, or prompts new insights. If desired, consult a trusted Bible commentary.
- Carefully read chapter 6 of *Sermon on the Mount*. Note any material you need or want to research further before the session.
- Have on hand a variety of Bible translations and trusted study Bibles and commentaries for participants to use (recommended).
- If using the DVD or streaming video in your study, preview the session 6 segment and choose the best time in your session to view it.
- Optional: Before the session, prepare the opening activity by standing two empty toilet paper or paper towel tubes upright at one end of a table (the longer the table, the better) just far enough apart for a small ball to roll cleanly between them.

As Your Group Gathers

Welcome participants. Ask those who attended the previous session to talk briefly about what most interested, challenged, or helped them.

Optional: Recruit volunteers to stand at one end of the table and roll the ball between the two tubes at the opposite end—the "narrow gate." You may want to award small candies or other inexpensive prizes to those who successfully roll the ball through the "gate" without knocking the tubes over.

Read aloud Matthew 7:13-14. Ask:

- What does Jesus mean by "the narrow gate"?
- How do we know whether we are on the road leading to the wide gate of "destruction" or the road leading to the narrow gate of "life"?

Read aloud from *Sermon on the Mount*: "Although the Sermon on the Mount begins with the Beatitudes and the promises of comfort, it moves inexorably to challenges to that comfort. Jesus is not selling his disciples a false hope; he is excruciatingly honest with them. . . . No one said the path into the kingdom would be easy." Tell participants they will explore various aspects of the challenging, narrow road into the kingdom of heaven in this final session.

Pray this prayer or one of your own:

> *God Most High, God Most Free: Throughout the ages, you have called your people to journey through this imperfect and broken world and through their own imperfect and broken lives toward the new, whole world you have promised. As we conclude our study of the Sermon on the Mount, may we sense your Spirit stirring us to continue our journeys, trusting you will not only guide us to the road that leads to life but also strengthen us to travel it, following in the footsteps of our great Teacher, Jesus Christ. Amen.*

Challenges on the Way to the Narrow Gate

For each of the sections below, recruit volunteers to read the Scripture cited, then lead a discussion using some or all of the questions provided. If you are leading a larger group, consider forming small teams and assigning each team a section to read and discuss.

Matthew 7:6

- AJ states this verse may sound, at first, like obvious advice. Why do you think Jesus gives it?
- "Despite claims by numerous sermons," writes AJ, "'dogs' does *not* mean 'Gentiles'; Jews did not typically call Gentiles 'dogs.' Nor did Jews, in general, find dogs to be unclean or disgusting animals." Why is it important to understand that Jesus is not calling non-Jews offensive animals in this saying?
- Interpreting this verse, AJ connects it to Jesus's parable of a precious pearl (Matthew 13:45-46) and comments, "Something so precious is not to be wasted." How do we proclaim the gospel widely but not wastefully?

- What other precious resources must we use wisely if we are to live into the kingdom of heaven?
- How can the community of faith help you use your precious resources more wisely?

Matthew 7:7-11

- For what do you think Jesus is expecting his disciples to ask, search, and knock? Why?
- AJ applies these words to relationships between members of Jesus's new community: "they can express their needs to others, who will answer; the homeless will find a home, and the hungry will find food. . . . They knock at the door of the family." How have you experienced your community of faith's willingness to answer the needs of those who knock at their doors?
- Commenting on verses 9-10, AJ notes, "Not all parents are responsible." How do you think people who have been abused and neglected as children would respond to Jesus's rhetorical question? What does or should your congregation do to demonstrate that in the kingdom of heaven, as AJ writes, "all children are fed and loved . . . [and] all adults are responsible and loving"?
- AJ also applies Jesus's words to his disciples' relationship to God: "If we ask God for forgiveness, that door will open." For what have you asked or sought from God? How, if at all, do you believe God has responded?
- Commenting on Jesus's characterization of his disciples as "evil" (v. 11), AJ writes, "Personally, I don't feel totally depraved, and personally, I don't think humanity is totally depraved either. . . . We are already aware that we are basically good people, and at the same time we are aware that, given the imperatives in the Sermon on the Mount, we can do better." Do you agree with this assessment of human goodness? Why or why not? Why do you think Jesus calls his disciples "evil" in this saying? (Compare, as AJ also does, Mark 10:18).

- AJ explains that Jesus is using a form of rabbinical argument called *qal v'homer*—"light and heavy." He has already used this type of argument in the Sermon (Matthew 6:26, 30). How do "light and heavy" arguments help us consider our lives from a perspective fit for the kingdom of heaven? How can the community of faith help maintain this perspective over the long haul of faithful discipleship?

Matthew 7:12

- Do you remember when you first learned the Golden Rule? Who taught it to you and why? Why do you think versions of it can be found in many cultures and religions?
- AJ points out that the Golden Rule is one of only two of Jesus's summaries of the Scriptures of Israel. Read the other in Matthew 22:34-40. How do the two summaries of Scripture clarify and complement each other?
- According to AJ, "the summary is the guide through which the rest of Torah, and Jesus's teachings, should be filtered." In your experience, how would consistently keeping Jesus's summaries of Torah in mind change how Christians understand and apply Scripture?
- AJ also discusses the "Silver Rule": "And what you hate, do not do to anyone" (Tobit 4:15). Like the Golden Rule, "it is a touchstone . . . by which all the other *mitzvot* (commandments) should be understood." How might both the Silver and Golden Rules be "deformed" and abused by taking them out of the larger context of Scripture as a whole?
- How can the community of faith help you abide by the Golden Rule?

Matthew 7:15-23

- "False prophets," writes AJ, "tend to be those who proclaim the wide gate and the easy road, or better, 'easy street.'" How can people of faith identify false prophets today—and how, if at all, should they respond to false prophets?

- "To say 'All you need to do is believe in Jesus and you will be saved' is to deform the gospel." Do you agree with AJ's assertion? Why or why not?

- Jesus says true and false prophets can be known "by their fruits" (vv. 16-20), but as AJ writes, "the good fruit is not always obvious." To what specific examples of the "good fruit" that the apostle Paul lists in Galatians 5:22-23 would you point to help other people of faith identify true prophets (messengers) from God?

- In verse 23, the New Revised Standard Version calls false prophets "evildoers," a word AJ states is better translated "[people] working lawlessness." How does or how should this condemnation of those who deny the validity of God's Law, or Torah, shape Christians' understanding of the church's Old Testament?

- "Leave the deeds of power, the 'mighty works,' to God," urges AJ; "instead, welcome the stranger. To do that is miracle enough." What other "miracles" of this kind—of everyday "good fruit"—have you experienced or participate in that led you to identify true prophets?

- How can the community of faith work together to better discern and respond to true and false prophets?

Closing Activity

Read aloud from *Sermon on the Mount*: "No one said the path into the kingdom would be easy But is it worthwhile? Absolutely, because it allows disciples to focus their love and their talents, to have better knowledge of self and better concepts of living within a community."

Ask:

- How has our study of the Sermon on the Mount given you better knowledge of yourself?

How has our study given you a better understanding of what life in Jesus's ideal community is like?

- How has our study given you new insight into who God is and God's will for your community of faith at this time?

Thank everyone for taking part in the study. Close the session by praying this prayer or one of your own:

> Lord Jesus, we would be not only hearers of your words but also doers. We would find and follow the road leading to your heavenly kingdom, the road you walked before us, narrow and difficult though it is. Bless this season of study we have finished. By your power, may it move us to a continued life of action, living ever more faithfully as your ideal community, showing ever more clearly the glory and love of our Father and yours to the world. Amen.

Exchange signs and words of peace with one another as the group departs.

Made in the USA
Monee, IL
25 February 2022